P9-BJX-880

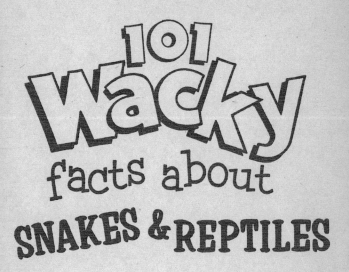

101 Wacky facts about SNAKES & REPTILES

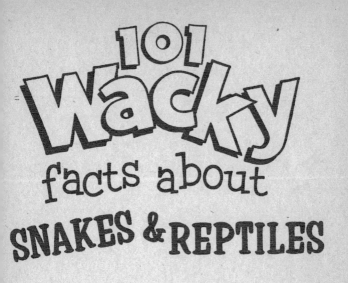

101 Wacky facts about SNAKES & REPTILES

BY WALTER RETAN

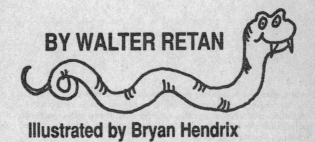

Illustrated by Bryan Hendrix

A Parachute Press Book

SCHOLASTIC INC.
New York Toronto London Auckland Sydney

No part of this publication may be reproduced in whole or in part, or stored in a
retrieval system, or transmitted on any form or by any means, electronic,
mechanical, photocopying, recording, or otherwise, without written permission of
the publisher. For information regarding permission, write to Scholastic, Inc., 730
Broadway, New York, NY 10003.

ISBN 0-590-44891-9

Copyright © 1991 by Parachute Press Inc.
All rights reserved. Published by Scholastic Inc.

Designed by Paula Jo Smith

12 11 10   5 6/9

Printed in the U. S. A.   01

First Scholastic printing, November 1991

THE SCALIEST
ANIMALS ALIVE!

Talk about family ties! Did you know that the giant dinosaurs that lived millions of years ago were members of the reptile family? Snakes, alligators, turtles, and lizards are reptiles also.

What happens when a reptile gets too cold? It can't move, that's what! Reptiles are cold-blooded. This means their body temperature stays about the same as the temperature of the air around them. If it gets too cold, they don't have the energy to move.

TYRANNOSAURUS REX

That's why so many reptiles live in warm countries. If it gets too hot, they can cool off by hiding under a rock or in a cave, but at least they can move!

No sweat! . . . at least for reptiles. Their scales are designed to keep water in their bodies.

IT'S HISS-TERICAL!

A snake "walks" on its ribs! The snake grips the ground with the sharp edges of the scales (scutes) that cover the underside of its body. Muscles inside its body pull it along the ground. The rougher the ground, the faster the snake can travel.

The paradise tree snake glides through the air from one branch to another, and sometimes from one tree to another. How does it do this? By flinging itself out from a branch, keeping its body in an S-shape, and trapping air in a hollow created on the underside of its body. This cushion of air acts as a parachute—it slows the snake's drop to a lower branch!

Snakes have no eyelids! That's why they always seem to be staring at you. They don't mean to be impolite! They even sleep with their eyes open.

If you want to fool a snake . . . stay very silent and still. Snakes can't focus their eyes well. They can see movement easily, but it's hard for them to recognize a nonmoving object.

Snakes need glasses. But actually they *do* wear spectacles! A transparent scale covers a snake's eyes in order to protect it. This is called a "spectacle"!

Did you ever wonder why a snake keeps flicking its forked tongue back and forth? Although snakes have nostrils, they do a lot of their smelling with their tongues. The tongue picks up scent particles in the air and on the ground.

A special organ called *Jacobson's organ* receives the scent particles from the tongue. It contains nerve endings that are very sensitive to smells. By using its tongue, a snake can recognize its mate, locate food, or spot an enemy.

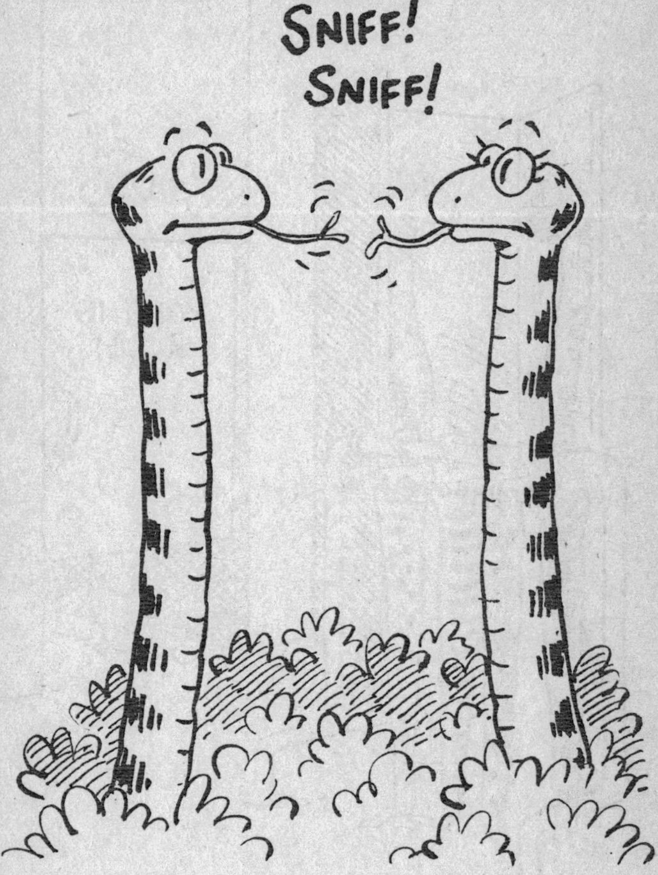
SNIFF!
SNIFF!

Snakes don't have any outer ear openings—they pick up vibrations in the ground through their skulls. But they do have an inner ear through which they hear a limited range of sounds.

Rub a dub dub . . . every so often a snake sheds its skin. It rubs its nose and mouth against a stone, and keeps rubbing until it makes a little hole in its skin. Then the snake begins to push itself very slowly through the hole, crawling right out of the old skin. This is called "molting."

Under the old, worn skin there's a brand-new one. Even the spectacles that protect a snake's eyes are new!

The average human has 33 bones in his or her backbone. The reticulated python has 400 bones! That's why a snake can twist itself into coils, and you can't!

SNACKS FOR SNAKES

Snakes can go several months without eating! Because they are cold-blooded, they don't need to burn up a lot of food to keep warm. When they start getting thin, they'll go hunting again.

Would you want to train a snake? Good luck! Usually animal trainers can get animals to do things by rewarding them with food. But snakes have such irregular eating habits that a reward of food just doesn't interest them.

Would you like to cuddle with a snake? Be careful! Pythons and boas kill their victims by coiling their bodies around them. They squeeze the captured animal until it can't breathe anymore.

Snakes swallow their victims whole! A snake's sharp, pointed teeth curve back toward its throat, so they're no good for chewing!

Small constricting snakes are content to wrap themselves around little animals like mice, rats, birds, and frogs. But a 20- to 30-foot African python will sometimes kill and swallow a small deer!

How does the snake keep from choking to death when swallowing its prey? A snake may take a half hour or more to swallow a large animal. Many kinds of snakes can push their windpipes forward over their tongues and out their mouths. This movable windpipe allows the snake to keep breathing while its mouth is stuffed full!

Sometimes snakes get really greedy! If a king snake has a chance to catch more than one mouse at a time, it will hold one tight in its coils until it finishes eating the other one! It doesn't intend to let its "second course" get away!

The tiny threadsnake, the smallest snake in the world, eats mostly termites. It has such a little mouth that it sucks the insides out of the insect's body and leaves the rest of the termite on the ground!

Over easy! That's the way the African egg eater likes its eggs. This snake lives in trees, where it searches for eggs in birds' nests. Sometimes the eggs are twice as wide as the snake's body. This doesn't stop the snake—it simply stretches its jaws to the limit and slowly pulls its mouth *over* the egg! Sharp, spinelike bones in the snake's throat pierce the egg as it slides down. The liquid part of the egg runs down into the stomach, while the snake spits out the shell. Egg eaters don't seem to like eggshells any more than we do!

Years ago farmers believed that milk snakes liked to roam around barns and cowsheds so that they could suck the milk out of cows! Actually they live around barns because they like to eat mice.

It's a snake eat snake world! Some snakes often eat other snakes, but the California king snake makes a specialty of it. It will even eat a rattlesnake. Fortunately for the king snake, it is immune to a rattlesnake's poison!

HOLLYWOOD

SURF

29

Have you heard the story of the two-headed king snake? Believe it or not, a few freaky two-headed snakes have been born! This particular snake lived in the San Diego Zoo. Since king snakes like to eat other snakes, this two-headed snake had a real problem. One of its heads tried to swallow the other! The zookeeper rescued the attacked head, but later the rescued head must have decided to get even. It attacked the first head! And that was the end of the two-headed snake!

THE BITE THAT KILLS!

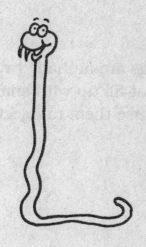

Did you know that some snakes have their very own poison factory? A snake's poison is made in two special glands in its head. Two tubes connect the glands to the fangs. The poison runs through these tubes and into the fangs.

Fangs are actually two hollow teeth that fill up with snake poison! Snakes use them to inject or spit poison.

The fangs of rattlesnakes, cottonmouth moccasins, and other vipers are so long that they have to fold back against the roofs of their mouths when not in use.

The rattlesnake's warning of attack is a rattling sound created by the hard rings at the end of its tail. The hard rings hit against each other, making this rattling sound. If surprised or threatened, a rattlesnake will shake its tail very fast.

Every time a rattlesnake sheds its skin, it gets a new ring on its rattler!

Guess how the deadly cotton-mouth moccasin snake got its name. When it opens its jaws wide, its mouth looks as if it's lined with soft, white cotton!

The most feared poisonous snake in Africa is the black mamba—just *two drops* of venom from its fangs can kill a human being.

The black mamba isn't black at all. It's a kind of gray-brown.

A black mamba *baby* snake may only weigh about an ounce, but it too can inject poison with its tiny fangs— enough poison to kill a mouse!

In India snake charmers claim they can train cobras to dance to the music they play on their flutes. Actually the snakes can't even hear the music! They are just following the swaying movements of the snake charmer and his flute.

The king cobra is the biggest and deadliest poisonous snake. It has a hood of loose skin attached to long ribs just below its head. When a cobra is getting ready to strike, it raises its head and the hood of skin opens out much like an umbrella. This makes the snake look twice as big.

What a bluffer! The hognose snake has no poison and it doesn't bite. But when an enemy threatens it, the hognose puffs up its head and throat, hisses, and then lunges at the enemy with its mouth wide open.

If this tactic doesn't work, the hognose suddenly flops over on its back and plays dead!

The rubber boa has another way of dealing with enemies. It coils in a ball, hiding its head beneath its body. Then it raises the blunt end of its tail, which looks just like its head, and waves it back and forth. If an enemy attacks the false head, the real head remains safely out of sight!

40

The spitting cobra of Africa squirts a fine stream of venom at its enemy's face. The cobra squeezes the venom out through pinholes in the front of its fangs. The poison doesn't kill, but it causes pain and eye damage— sometimes even permanent blindness.

The spitting cobra can spit its poison a distance of eight or nine feet! If it spits six times, it will run out of venom, but by the next day it will have manufactured a new supply.

THE AMAZING LIZARD!

Lizards are close relatives of snakes Most of them have a head, a body, four legs, and a tail, but a few kinds are legless.

How can you tell the difference between a snake and a legless lizard? Lizards have movable eyelids, as well as outer ear openings. Snakes don't have either of them.

Lizards molt—have a change of skin—just like snakes, except that a snake sheds its skin in one piece, while a lizard's old skin comes off in strips and patches.

Glass snakes aren't snakes at all—they really should be called glass lizards! But because they don't have any legs and their tails are twice as long as their bodies, they're frequently mistaken for snakes.

Tricky tricky! If an enemy grabs a glass lizard by its long, brittle tail, this lizard simply sheds its tail and crawls away! The tail keeps right on wiggling, and the enemy keeps on fighting with it!

The glass lizard—like many other lizards—will then grow another tail. But the new tail won't be as long as the old one.

The worm lizard looks like a giant earthworm. It can grow to a length of ten inches, but its body is only one quarter of an inch thick.

Ants beware! Worm lizards have no legs, and they're blind. They live underground, using their strong shovel-shaped heads to tunnel through the earth in search of termites and ants.

There's one lizard that can fly for distances of 50 feet. It's called a flying lizard. It has flaps of folded skin on each side of its short, thin body. By moving long, flexible rib bones attached to its flaps, this lizard turns them into "wings."

When a basilisk lizard is frightened, it gets up on its hind legs and runs. It can even run across water! It moves so fast on its long fringed toes that it doesn't have time to sink down into the water.

The frilled lizard is a comical reptile that lives in Australia. If attacked, it rears up on its hind legs and spreads an enormous frill out on each side of its head. Then it opens its mouth wide and hisses.

The horned toad is really a lizard. It has a toadlike shape and face, but its body is covered with short sharp spines.

When a horned lizard is frightened, it can squirt blood from the corners of each eye up to a distance of three feet!

The least gecko is the smallest reptile in the world—and definitely among the noisiest! These tiny lizards chirp and bark like old gossips.

Tree geckos have many tiny nooks in their footpads that enable them to scamper up and down tree trunks or climb over log fences!

Some geckos have slits on their toes that act as little suction pads. These geckos can run up a smooth pane of glass or even walk across a ceiling upside down!

Crunch, crunch, crunch—geckos are wonderful cockroach hunters. Sometimes people keep them in their homes for this purpose. It isn't very pleasant, however, to hear them crunching their victims between their jaws at night!

Marine iguanas are the best swimmers of all the lizards. They'd better be—their favorite food is seaweed!

Marine iguanas are really quite shy and would never harm anybody. But if humans come near them, they puff a kind of steam through their noses. They look scary enough to keep most people away!

The Komodo dragon of Indonesia is the biggest lizard in the world. It grows to be as long as a cow—nine to ten feet—but it has very short legs, so it isn't nearly as tall!

Although a Komodo dragon can weigh as much as 300 pounds when fully grown, it will sometimes climb a tree!

Komodo dragons are lazy hunters! Although they hunt and eat deer, wild pigs, and monkeys, they prefer munching on animals that are already dead! Apparently these are easier to tear apart and digest.

There are 3,000 kinds of lizards, but only two are poisonous—the Gila monster and the Mexican beaded lizard.

The Gila monster doesn't have fangs like a poisonous snake. Instead, its sharp-edged, grooved teeth deliver the venom at the same time the lizard bites down. The poison paralyzes its victims!

Fortunately for us, Gila monsters are very shy, grow no longer than two feet, and almost never attack people!

What do a Gila monster and a camel have in common? When the Gila monster eats a lot, its tail gets very thick from storing up fat—just like a camel's hump!

Hold on tight! The jaws of both a Mexican beaded lizard and a Gila monster are strong and hard to dislodge when they bite.

A LIZARD OF MANY COLORS

The chameleon is best known for the way it can change color. Its nervous system and hormones seem to control the changes.

You name it, the chameleon does it! If the chameleon is afraid, it will change color rapidly. If it's too hot or too cold, it will turn lighter or darker. Different color combinations and patterns mean different moods. Sometimes a change of color helps a chameleon to blend in better with its surroundings!

You might call it a cross-eyed lizard! The African chameleon has incredible eyes that bulge out on scaly turrets at either side of its head. Each eye can rotate independently—the left eye may be looking down at an insect, while the right eye is looking up at a flying bird!

A chameleon's feet are perfect for a tree dweller. The five toes are joined together in two bunches—one on the inside of the foot, the other on the outside. The chameleon uses these two bunches of toes to clamp onto a branch or twig. Its grip is so powerful that it can even hang upside down.

If the chameleon should happen to lose its grip, it always has a back-up—its tail! Chameleon tails are prehensile, like monkey tails. They can wrap them tightly around a branch and swing through the air.

Here's a great way to catch your dinner! The chameleon's tongue is as long as its body and tail put together, and it can shoot out of its mouth with amazing speed! The sticky mucus at the end of its tongue latches onto insects and holds them fast until the chameleon pulls its tongue back into its mouth.

LOGS WITH JAWS

There were crocodiles living millions of years ago when dinosaurs roamed the earth. Fossils show that some crocodiles living then grew to be as long as a city bus! Fortunately, today's crocodiles aren't even half that long.

Crocodiles, alligators, and their close relatives are called crocodilians. They live in or near water in warm regions of the world.

Why are crocodiles and alligators called logs with jaws? Because when they swim along the surface of the water, their rough skin and long cigar shape make them look like huge floating logs. But watch out . . . these logs have a deadly bite!

How quaint! Alligators and crocodiles like to drag their unlucky victims underwater in order to drown them before eating them.

Most reptiles make very little noise. Many are completely silent. But the crocodilians are different. They can make a very loud noise that sounds like a deep roar.

One thing you can be sure of. A crocodilian will never stick its tongue out at you. They have immovable tongues.

Stones for dinner? Crocodiles sometimes swallow pebbles, which they carry in their stomachs. Scientists used to believe that these pebbles helped to grind and digest their food. Now many of them think the weight of the stones may help the crocodiles stay underwater—or even walk on the river bottom!

African crocodiles like to lie in the sun along muddy riverbanks with their mouths wide open!

While the crocodile lies there with its mouth open on the riverbank, a small African bird called a "plover" often lands on the crocodile's lower jaw and pecks bits of food and insects from its mouth!

The crocodiles must appreciate these little birds—or should we call them "living toothbrushes"? They never try to eat them.

Have you ever heard of a gavial? This close cousin of the crocodile lives in the rivers of India. Gavials have more than 100 sharp, even teeth. Fortunately for us, their favorite food is fish!

Gavials are champion underwater swimmers. Special flaps cover their nostrils and a kind of valve shuts off the windpipe so that a gavial can open its mouth to catch fish without swallowing a lot of water.

Caimans are also related to alligators. They are very bold—they're not even afraid to hunt and eat the fierce meat-eating piranha fish that swim in tropical rivers!

There's one reptile that's not afraid to attack a caiman. Giant anaconda snakes have been known to catch, squeeze, and swallow a six-foot caiman with no trouble at all! That "snack" will last the greedy snake for several weeks.

HAVE SHELL, WILL TRAVEL

MOBILE HOME PARK

The only reptiles that have shells are turtles! Most kinds of turtles can pull their head, legs, and tail into their shell. It serves as a suit of armor, keeping the turtle safe from its enemies.

Turtles don't have any teeth. Instead they have a beak with a hard, sharp edge that they use to cut their food.

A tortoise is a turtle that lives on land. Tortoises have short stumpy legs that look like a smaller version of an elephant's legs.

The largest tortoises in the world measure up to four feet long and weigh as much as 600 pounds!

What a stinkpot! Musk turtles have something better than their shells to protect them. When disturbed, they give off a *baaad*-smelling liquid from special glands.

Baby stinkpots are so tiny you could fit more than six in your hand. But first put a clothespin on your nose!

Most land turtles lumber along very slowly, but a few can move with surprising speed. The smooth softshell turtle has even been known to outrun a man on level ground!

The matamata turtle of Brazil is the world's oddest-looking turtle. Its shell is covered with bumps on which tiny green plants (algae) grow. Long tassels of skin, looking just like weeds, hang from its neck.

Curiosity killed the fish! The matamata has such a long neck and snout that it can rest on the muddy river bottom and yet keep its nostrils out of the water in order to breathe. It stays perfectly motionless while fish swim up, attracted by what seems to be a pile of leaves and plants. But suddenly, the matamata opens its mouth and sucks in one of the curious fish. It not only swallows the fish but squirts out a mouthful of water all at the same time!

The world's laziest fisherman is probably the alligator snapping turtle. It sits quietly on the bottom of a creek with its mouth wide open. Nothing moves except its wriggling, fleshy pink tongue. Hungry fish swim closer and closer. To them the tongue must look just like a juicy worm. But instead of catching a worm, the poor fish gets caught between the turtle's jaws!

The flesh of the hawksbill turtle can be poisonous to humans, perhaps because these turtles often eat jellyfish—poisonous stingers and all!

TURTLES WITH FLIPPERS

The biggest turtle in the world is the leatherback. This giant sea turtle can grow to be eight feet long and weigh as much as 1,500 pounds! It's called a leatherback because the upper layer of its shell is made of a heavy, leathery skin.

The biggest turtles live in the sea. Sea turtles don't have legs like land turtles. Instead, they have boardlike flippers that are too stiff to pull into their shells.

Sea turtles beat their flippers when they swim in much the same way that birds flap their wings when they fly!

The green and the leatherback turtles are the fastest swimmers. With their large, strong flippers, they can swim at speeds as fast as 20 miles an hour. That's about four times as fast as an Olympic swimmer's speed!

Free ride anyone? Sea turtles like to float on top of the water, letting the rays from the bright tropical sun warm their shells. Sometimes, while the turtle is sunbathing, a brown booby bird lands on its back and gets a free ride!

Green turtles aren't green at all! Their shells are brownish with yellow lines. So why call them "green" turtles? Because their fat turns a greenish color when their meat is cooked for soup.

In the 1400s and 1500s, when Columbus and other explorers were sailing the oceans, they had no way to carry fresh meat on their ships. Green turtles solved their problem.

The sailors caught green turtles alive and turned them over on their backs aboard ship so they couldn't walk around. By keeping the turtles moist, the sailors could be sure of a fresh meat supply for several months!

If green turtles didn't make such delicious soup, more of them would be alive today.

The flesh of leatherback turtles has such a revolting taste that they don't have to worry about being turned into soup!

OH, BABY!

Some female snakes and lizards lay eggs while others give birth to living young. Baby snakes and lizards can get out of their eggs without any help at all.

Snakes have a special little egg tooth on their upper jaw that can saw right through the shell. The babies shed this tooth as soon as they get out of the egg!

The female python lays anywhere from ten to a thousand eggs in a nest! This snake mother actually incubates her eggs by curling up around the eggs in order to keep them warm.

Where's mommy? Every baby snake and lizard is on its own just as soon as it is born. Their mother has nothing to do with them—her job is finished as soon as she lays her eggs!

Every two or three years female sea turtles return to the land where they were born. There, they lay their eggs. Sometimes they travel as far as 1,400 miles—a trip that may take them across an entire ocean and last for three months!

What a nose! Scientists think that the sea turtle's keen sense of smell helps it to return to the beach where it was born.

Sometimes hundreds of mother turtles gather on one nesting beach. They scoop holes in the sand, lay their eggs, and carefully cover the holes with sand. A female may lay as many as 100 eggs!

When the baby sea turtles hatch, they almost immediately head for the water. How do they know in which direction to go? Scientists think they are attracted by the light reflections on the water!

SLOW POKE

What is a tuatara? This reptile is absolutely unique. It's been around, *unchanged*, for at least 200 million years! The tuatara is the only survivor of an ancient group of reptiles that lived in the days of the dinosaurs!

Tuataras can be found on just a few cold, rocky islands off the coast of New Zealand. Though they can remain active in much colder temperatures than other reptiles, they do everything *very* slowly.

A tuatara takes only about ten breaths of air an hour! Sometimes it will go without breathing for a whole hour!

A tuatara's eggs take about a year to develop inside the mother's body. After she finally lays them, they take another year to hatch!

Tuataras sleep during the day. At night they creep around very slowly searching for worms, beetles, and small birds and lizards.

Tuataras grow very, very slowly, and they don't mate until they are 20 years old. All in all, they act as if they know that they are the oldest surviving reptiles!